Churchill

Seasons of the Moon
SPRING MOON

ALSO BY JEAN CRAIGHEAD GEORGE

ONE DAY IN THE DESERT

ONE DAY IN THE PRAIRIE

ONE DAY IN THE TROPICAL RAIN FOREST

ONE DAY IN THE WOODS

SHARK BENEATH THE REEF

THE TALKING EARTH

THE TARANTULA IN MY PURSE

THERE'S AN OWL IN THE SHOWER

WATER SKY

WHO REALLY KILLED COCK ROBIN?
AN ECO MYSTERY

Seasons of the Moon

SPRING MOON

JEAN CRAIGHEAD GEORGE

♛ HARPERTROPHY®
AN IMPRINT OF HARPERCOLLINSPUBLISHERS

Spring Moon
Copyright © 2002 by Julie Productions, Inc.
Originally published as individual volumes:
The Moon of the Salamanders text copyright © 1967, 1992
by Jean Craighead George
The Moon of the Chickarees text copyright © 1969, 1992
by Jean Craighead George
The Moon of the Monarch Butterflies text copyright © 1968, 1993
by Jean Craighead George

Library of Congress Cataloging-in-Publication Data
George, Jean Craighead, 1919–
    Spring moon / Jean Craighead George. — 1st Harper Trophy ed.
      p.   cm. — (Seasons of the moon ; 3)
    Works originally published from 1967–1969 in series: The Thirteen
moons.
    Includes bibliographical references.
    Contents: The moon of the salamanders — The moon of the
chickarees — The moon of the monarch butterflies.
    ISBN 0-06-442171-6 (pbk.)
    1. Salamanders—Juvenile literature.   2. Tamiasciurus—Juvenile
literature.   3. Monarch butterfly—Juvenile literature.   4. Spring—
Juvenile literature.   [1. Salamanders.   2. Red squirrels.   3. Squirrels.
4. Monarch butterfly.   5. Butterflies.]   I. Title.
QL668.C2 G45   2002   2001024641
591.4'3—dc21   CIP
                                                          AC

Book design by Andrea Simkowski
❖
First Harper Trophy edition, 2002
Visit us on the World Wide Web!
www.harperchildrens.com

CONTENTS

WHY IS THIS SERIES CALLED
SEASONS OF THE MOON?

Each year there are either thirteen full or thirteen new moons. This series is named in honor of the four seasons of the thirteen moons of the year.

Our culture, which bases its calendar year on sun-time, has no names for the thirteen moons. I have named the thirteen lunar months after thirteen North American animals. Primarily night prowlers, these animals, at a particular time of the year in a particular place, do wondrous things. The places are known to you, but the animal moon names are not because I made them up. So that you can place them on our sun calendar, I have identified them with the names of our months. When I ran out of these, I gave the thirteenth moon, the Moon of the Moles, the expandable name December–January.

Fortunately, the animals do not need calendars, for names or no names, sun-time, or moon-time, they follow their own inner clocks.

—JEAN CRAIGHEAD GEORGE

Seasons of the Moon
SPRING MOON

THE MOON OF THE
SALAMANDERS

In the third moon of the year the first thaw came. Warm winds blew for days and nights. Lakes of ice turned to water. The snow slipped away. The frost let go of the soil. The Northern Hemisphere was tilting into the sun, and even the polar winds could not stop the coming of spring. The warmth penetrated the dark, rich soil in Michigan and southern Canada and thawed the last holdouts of winter: the floors of the woodlands and their ephemeral ponds. Sequestered among old hemlocks and maples, beeches and oaks, these ponds, unlike lakes and permanent ponds, are here in March, gone in August.

The first spring thaw was followed by the first spring rain. Water poured from the clouds. The cold ponds filled to their brims and set a dark stage for the ancient ritual of the mole salamanders, one of the seven families, or groups, of salamanders that live in North America, the continent where most of the salamanders dwell.

From looking at fossils, we know that one billion three hundred million years ago, limy sea plants developed in the seas. Some five hundred million years ago, shellfish and other animals without backbones evolved. They were followed by fishlike creatures that did have backbones. In another 60 million years plants appeared on the land. Sea scorpions were large and numerous, and countless kinds of shelled animals dwelled in the primitive oceans. When another 30 million years had passed, fishes were common in salt and fresh water. The first forests flourished in vast swamps. Into this lush landscape evolved the amphibians, animals who dared to come ashore for part of their lives. They were followed by land animals, insects, reptiles, small dinosaurs, birds, big dinosaurs, as well as the flowering plants. A mere 60 million years ago, the first mammals, characterized by hair and warm blood, developed among the feet of massive horned and armored dinosaurs. The early mammals were small and awkward, but like the fish and birds, the reptiles and sea creatures, they changed and evolved. The plants also changed and evolved, as did the land and atmosphere.

But not the salamanders. Hidden in the darkness of the earth, in caves, under rocks and logs, most moving only in the blackest hours of night, they have remained unchanged for some 330 million years. The salamanders today look like the first salamanders on earth.

Like those first salamanders, they still have soft legs, clawless toes, moist bodies, and eyes that do not move. The grooves along the sides of their bodies have been passed unchanged from generation to generation. They still live part of their life in water and part on land, as do the other amphibians, the frogs and toads.

The spotted salamander, a handsome member of the mole salamander family, dwells in the dark, wet soil from the Gaspé Peninsula to central Ontario and south to Georgia and Texas. Every year in the north, on the night of the first spring rain after the first spring thaw, the spotted salamanders come out of hibernation. They act out a strange and ancient drama just as they did 330 million years ago.

One of these actors awoke under the soil in a woodland in Michigan. Like all mole salamanders, he was a creature of the darkness. He lifted his head and heard the thaw. It purled. He listened to the rain. It tapped.

He listened. He did not listen with ears on the outside of his head, for he had none, but with primitive ears that lay inside the head and along his body and tail, much like the hearing organs of the fishes. These "body ears" pick up subtle sounds in the water and the earth. He heard the tapping of the rain. It grew heavier. The spotted salamander pushed up on his short, soft legs and stepped forward. He moved slowly and awkwardly, for he was not well adapted for walking on land.

He was big, almost nine inches long, and between fifteen and twenty-five years old. Not only did he look like his early ancestors, he behaved like them. He ate insects and worms, and he lived in earthen darkness as they did. Like them he returned to the water once a year on the night of the first spring rain after the first spring thaw. This was his night to go.

Slowly, the salamander walked to the edge

of the log under which he lived. Light-yellow spots lined either side of his black body from his eyes to the tip of his tail. His belly was slate gray. He was missing a left toe, but he would not be crippled for long. Salamanders can regenerate lost feet, toes, and tails.

At the edge of his log he felt the night air. He listened to the tap of the rain. The tap became a spurtle, then a roar. Water cascaded over his log, soaked him, and gave him courage. He strode out into the night.

Half swimming, half slithering, he moved across the woodland floor. After a short distance his swishing tail touched a wood snail, coiled deep in its shell. The salamander paused. His body had heard small scratching noises inside the wood snail's shell, sounds so small only a salamander could hear them.

The scratching sound was the snail opening its winter doors. When cold weather had arrived last fall, the snail had pulled into its shell. It had rested and laid down a layer of calcium and then pulled further in. It then laid down another layer of calcium. Eventually it was sealed deep in its shell for the winter.

A few days ago the snail had felt the warming of the earth and had begun unlocking its doors with thrusts and pushes. When the salamander's tail struck, the wood snail stopped unlatching, fearful that the thump might be an enemy.

The salamander, upon hearing no more sounds from the shell, pushed on through the rain. The snail slid its foot out, then its head, unfolded its long eye stalks, and looked upon the watery shapes on the lowly landscape. To learn more about them it pushed one of its soft antennae out of its head. It felt pummeling rain, pulled back into its shell, and shut its door. It was a land snail, not a water snail.

The salamander liked the rain. Each torrent of water was transportation for him. When a rivulet washed over him, he would be picked up and carried closer to his destination. One gush of rainwater swept him over the budding fiddleheads of a wood fern and the hump of a first bloodroot stalk. When he was finally dropped on the wet leaves, he lifted his blunt nose, took a bearing, and tramped on.

Other spotted salamanders felt the call of the moon of March. From under logs and stones, up from root-deep hideouts and buried dens, they emerged by the hundreds in the Michigan woods. A slithering parade, they moved downhill with the runoff.

From a hollow of a sugar maple tree, a screech owl saw the salamander swishing along in the parade. He was a tempting meal for the owl, but not tonight. Even a hungry screech owl would not fly in this downpour.

Tree trunks were waterfalls, rock surfaces were cascades, and leaf dams created lakes. The owl retreated into his dry hollow. The salamander trod on.

The spotted salamander swung his head and tail as he moved. When he was halfway down the hill, a dam of leaves broke behind him and a deluge of water picked him up and swept him around a rock.

He paddled his feet and tail and swam. On the far side of the rock, the water spread out, soaked into the ground, and vanished. He was dumped on the forest floor. He paused to take in the sounds and tastes of the night and quickly sensed he was facing in the wrong direction. Feeling the call of water to his right, he turned and walked downhill. Behind him came the silent parade of marching salamanders, their wet bodies shining in the rain.

Another leaf dam broke. The water rushed

beside him. On it floated a struggling case-bearer moth. The moth had spent the winter as a larva inside a silk-and-leaf-reinforced case he had made. When the air had grown cool last autumn, he had fastened the case to the bark of a wild cherry tree and crawled in for the winter. Just before the salamander awoke from hibernation, the young moth emerged from his case. He fought his way out and rested. His wings unfolded. His feet hardened. His antennae feathered out. He was ready to fly when the rain struck. Water rolled down the tree trunk and washed him into the woods, where he crawled onto a dam made of leaves. He was preparing to fly when it broke.

He went rushing past the salamander. Although he was salamander food, the long, chunky amphibian ignored him and strode on.

The salamander's four-toed front foot pushed back a leaf and uncovered the tip of a spring beauty. This forest flower raced to bloom before the tree leaves emerged and cast it in shade. Other spring flowers were hurrying to bloom. Two of them were the marsh marigolds in the wooded wetlands and the hepatica of the hillsides. The hepatica, a shiny-leafed plant, had not died in the winter. It had just stopped growing. When the warmth returned, it proceeded to grow again as if winter had never happened.

The salamander pushed against a hepatica leaf and thumped on. He did not see the plant, for salamander eyes see only things that move. They cannot see still objects.

The eyes of the salamander do not rotate, like the eyes of the mammals and birds, an attribute that helps creatures to see inanimate objects. To a salamander, if a moth does not move, a worm wiggle, or a leaf twist, then the world is a blank piece of paper. With the water moving an acorn along, the salamander saw it. Not only did he see the nut, but a worm on the nut. The worm was the larva of an acorn borer. It had wiggled out of the acorn when the flood struck and was now riding the rapids to somewhere.

Although the salamander would have snapped up the worm at any other time, he was not interested now. He had come to the edge of the woodland pond. It was the same pond to which he and his ancestors had come every year on the night of the first rain after the first spring thaw. The pond was a transient ecosystem. It dried up in summer.

The shallow pond water was black with tannin from the leaves. Because the pond dried up in summer, no fish could live in it. Without these predators to devour them, many delicate and remarkable creatures, including the salamanders, could live out their water lives in safety here.

The pond had a voice. It was the weeping of rain on water. The salamander remembered the voice and walked toward it. Suddenly he was swimming. He was a water creature again.

Small animals swirled around him, but they were too small for the salamander to see. They had awakened from winter's hibernation and were traveling about the pond. Some whipped past him flapping hairlike cilia. Others floated and wiggled their one-celled bodies. The pond teemed with life, but unlike the permanent ponds that held many different species, the transient ponds harbored only a few varieties—microscopic life, little crustaceans, a few changeling insects, and the amphibians. Transient ponds held few species, but many of each.

A black canoe-shaped whirligig beetle popped up from his hibernation place in the mud and rested on the surface. He sat very still looking in two directions with his four eyes. Two eyes looked up into the air, two looked down into the water. The beetle's ability to see in both the water and the air, as well as up and down, was the perfect solution for a creature that lives on the surface of the water where enemies and food come from both above and below.

Passing the spinning whirligig, the salamander looked at him and swam on. The movements of his legs and his body, so clumsy on land, were now as graceful as circling smoke. He turned his head and spiraled to the bottom of the pond.

Other salamanders had joined him. They rolled, circled, and arched as they began the ancient spring dance of the spotted salamanders.

The salamander dived over a floating oak leaf and swam down among a gathering of fairy shrimp. These beautiful red-and-blue crustaceans are distant relatives of the lobsters and crayfish. They are creatures of the spring, existing only in the transient ponds where fish cannot eat them. Seeing the salamander, they darted away on their backs, their hearts and stomachs visible through their glittering, transparent bodies. One hid behind a stick. Her black eyes, large for her tiny body, shone brightly on their little stalks. The tiny creature was on her back, for fairy shrimp live and travel feet up. She waved her "leaf-feet" gills, through which she breathed. She also used them to swim. The leaf-feet also operate like fingers and teeth. They pick up one-celled animals and plants, chew them with the gnawing tips and put them in the tiny mouth.

The salamander came up under the fairy shrimp, saw her slender heart beating in her glassy body, and swam on.

He was not interested in the fairy shrimp, or the hundreds of other little female fairy shrimp who were carrying their eggs in pockets on their bellies. In the salamander's pond there were only a few male fairy shrimp and sometimes none at all. Consequently, most of the eggs the female carried were not fertilized. Yet they would develop and grow in the mysterious way of nature called parthenogenesis. Under the moons of April and May, the fairy shrimp eggs, fertilized and unfertilized, would fall from the brood pockets of the females and sink to the bottom of the pond. When August dried up the pond, they would become "resting eggs," eggs that estivate, the summer equivalent of hibernate, through the heat and drought. When the water returned in the spring they would hatch into fairy shrimp larvae and mature with the thaw. The crystalline adults would swim with the salamanders, the one-celled animals and plants, and the whirligigs, in a celebration of the return of the transient pond.

The salamander danced on. He passed close to the pond's edge. A spring peeper, the tiniest frog in the forest, sat upon a stick. The peeper did not move. He had just awakened, and he was still too cold to hop. He was waiting for the earth to warm several more degrees; then he would leap along the pond edge and sing the first spring song of the frogs.

In the mud and leaves below the peeper sat the next frog to come out of hibernation, the wood frog. He was huddled down in the cold leaves, also silent and still. He needed more heat than the peeper to start him singing.

The salamander swam out from the shore. A female came toward him. They met. For a moment they drifted with their forearms and legs outspread; then the male circled her, twisting and rolling. The female swam upward in graceful loops. Another female joined the dancers. Two more males crossed the pond and slowly circled the females.

For hours and hours they danced. As the moon passed its apogee behind a barricade of rain clouds, the ancient ballet approached the finale. The salamanders dived, spiraled, and drifted faster and faster. The yellow spots on their sides shone like lanterns in the water. The lanterns glowed at all levels—the bottom, the middle, and the surface.

Then the spotted salamander dove under his female, lifted her on his nose, and carried her into deep water. He clasped her with his front legs, then released her.

She drifted. He descended to the bottom of the pond and laid a small white object on a leaf. The object looked like a collar button. It was a spermatophore, the tip of which held the DNA code of the male spotted salamander, the magic that would start the growth of the next generation.

The button laid, the spotted salamander swam away. Slowly, quietly, the female drifted down upon it, and the spermatozoa entered her body. The button remained on the leafy bottom.

The dance was done. The spotted salamander climbed ashore; the female surfaced, paddled to a leafy beach, and began walking back to her home.

The sky lightened above the Michigan woods. In the transient pond, white spermatophores grew dull, one-celled animals whipped their cilia, fairy shrimp swam on their backs, and whirligigs looked up and down. But there was not a salamander to be seen.

When the sun arose, the spotted salamander was in darkness under his log.

A sharp tap on the tree above him announced the arrival of morning. The downy woodpecker was chipping a nest hole. He did not work long. Nest building was just beginning, and like most beginnings in nature, it was slow. The woodpecker heard another woodpecker tapping. He flew off to see who it was. Neighbors were more important to the bird at this time of year than nest building.

He was setting up boundaries around his home and must check to make sure there were no trespassers.

The spotted salamander lay still in his dark world.

Just after daylight, the winds shook the trees, which trembled their roots and the earth around them. The salamander listened. The weather was changing. Cold air from the north had met the warm air above the thawed land, and the clash brewed turbulent gusts. The freeze would return. Snows would fall. The winter weather in Michigan had not come to an end.

The next night before the temperature dropped, the female salamander left her shelter under a stone and took the long road to the pond. Other females returned with her, and once more the spring pond became a stage for the salamanders.

The female circled and pirouetted until

she found a firm twig toward the middle of the pond where the water would not dry up too soon. She put her soft front legs around it. She pressed the five toes of her back feet against it. From her body spilled a mass of glittering black eggs.

At first the eggs were dots, round and tightly packed together. A thin layer of gelatinous material surrounded each egg. The material swelled when the eggs struck the water and formed a protective cover.

Her eggs clung to the stick just under the surface of the water. The female swam back to land and walked to her retreat. The transient pond would be mother to her offspring. It would keep them cool and moist. It would buoy the slender four-legged larvae that would hatch in May or June depending on the temperature of the water. It would give air to the gills that would stand up like ruffs behind their heads, and it would support the one-celled life

and the microscopic crustaceans that the salamander larvae would eat. They would grow
and thrive.

In August the salamander larvae, the fairy
shrimp, and the other changelings would be
ready for the drought. Just as the water was
about to vanish, the gills of the salamanders
would disappear, and the adult salamanders
would have air-breathing lungs. The timing of
the shift from water breathers to air breathers
would be perfect. As little adults they would
leave the pond and burrow into the moist leaves
and soil to live underground like their parents.

The fairy shrimp would also be prepared
for the drastic change—the adults would have
died, but not their resting eggs. The insects
would simply metamorphose and fly away.
The one-celled plants and animals would sur-
vive in the mud. The transient pond would be
asleep for the summer.

As the March moon waned, the salamander

heard spring noises in the soil around him. Beetle larvae were chewing roots; centipedes and sow bugs were hustling food. A chipmunk was digging a nursery in the ground far down below him. Getting to his feet, the salamander took a secret trail from his retreat to the underside of a stone. An earthworm wiggled. The salamander saw the worm, snapped it up, and ate.

The moon of the salamanders was done.

THE MOON OF THE CHICKAREES

The sun arose. The sky turned yellow. The faintest hint of green showed on the April land. A furry face appeared in the hollow of a fir tree. *"TCHER ~ r ~ r ~ r ~ r ~ r ~ r ~ rrrrr, TCHERRR ~ r ~ r ~ r ~ r ~ r ~ r!"* The screamer's breath turned to ice stars in the cold air.

She was an American red squirrel, about eleven inches long with rusty-brown fur and short tufts on her ears. She sported a bushy tail that was fringed with silver hairs. Her jet-black eyes were outlined in white.

She was mad. Her rights were being violated.

From the southern tip of the Appalachian Mountains to the coniferous forests of the West, and northward through Canada and Alaska, the red squirrels make their homes. They are the chatterboxes of the forests, screaming at bears, jays, magpies, woodpeckers, gray squirrels, house cats—an endless list— skunks, lynxes, and particularly each other. They are called "boomers" in the South and East, "bummers" on the Pacific Coast, and "chickarees" in New England and the West. Their loudest and most frantic noises are directed at the birds and beasts who would steal food from their storehouses, which are piles of green spruce and pine cones.

"TCHERrrrrrrrrrrr!" The chickaree in the hollow was screaming at the gray jaybird who was taking the berries she had dried and stored last summer under the bark of a tree. He paid her no heed.

"TCHER-RRRRRRRR," she screamed

louder. He spread his smoky gray wings, swallowed a berry, and chased a newly emerged beetle.

She protested again, then washed her face, brushed her ears, and looked down fourteen feet onto her small domain in the forest. It was only seventy feet across and sixty feet in length, but it was home and food and shelter—everything she needed for survival. It must be defended. The moon of April was rising, the moon of the rights of property owners.

"*TCHER-r-r-r,*" she called. She meant, "Get off my property!"

The chickaree's land lay along the Bitterroot River in Montana. Streams flowed into it from the Clearwater Mountains on the west and the Sapphire Mountains on the east. One of the streams, overflowing with snow melt this morning, cascaded through her property and spilled into the Bitterroot River. It made a gravel bar and a marsh where a huge moose browsed.

The chickaree screamed. Her cousin, and also her neighbor, was sneaking through last year's dried cow parsnips along the stream, to the tree where she stored her toadstools and mushrooms. Last autumn she had laid them out on a log, and when they were dry, she had hidden them under the bark of a limb on the old western hemlock.

Now they were about to be stolen, and she could do nothing about it. It was the first week in April, and she had just given birth to four babies, tiny, blind, and hairless. She could not leave them to chase her cousin. He picked up a mushroom, sat up, and stuffed it into one of his cheek pouches. Then he picked up another.

"TCHER-KERrrrr!" she exploded. So earsplitting was her cry that she startled the magpie in the river thicket nearby. The magpie,

a large black bird with white belly and shoulders and a long iridescent green tail, had returned to the Bitterroot after wandering east to Wisconsin for the winter. He was almost as talkative and noisy as the chickaree.

In a very loud voice he yakked, and flew after a trespassing magpie. It was the moon of property owners, and the magpie was asserting his rights.

The chickaree had her own trespasser. Once more she scolded her cousin, this time so fiercely that he jumped from the hemlock and landed on her favorite boulder. She screamed again. Flicking his elegant tail, he ran home.

She went back to her babies and pulled them into her belly fur. Gently she held them against the April cold. The frost had bitten the Bitterroot valley last night. It had also nipped the sprouting blades of winter grain as far south as Kansas and the buds of the cherry blossoms in faraway Michigan.

The chickaree knew nothing of these things. She knew only that her babies must be nurtured.

As the hours passed, the day warmed to a pleasant 40 degrees Fahrenheit, but the little squirrel was unaware of it; she was only aware of her suckling young. Their eyes were closed, and their tails and legs were so short that they did not even vaguely resemble their acrobatic father. The chickaree had mated with him early in March when the snow was falling softly. Now, forty days later, she was tending their babies, just as her mother had tended her a year ago. The chickaree did not remember her mother's tongue or her gentle paws. She did not remember being rolled on her back, tipped on her side, and bitten softly, although she was doing this to her babies. Vague memories and an inherited code of red squirrel behavior guided her in motherhood.

Like her own babies, she had nursed and slept on her first day of life. Ten days later, she was furry with velvety fuzz. In twenty-seven days, her eyes and ears opened. She was weaned in five weeks. Just before that day she and her brothers and sisters ventured out of the den. They clung to the limbs of their home tree and practiced running and balancing. After several days they could jump from limb to limb. Grasping small twigs, they swung and bounced in the sun-speckled shade. They went down to the ground on sunny days and, on rainy days, hid under logs. One day the chickaree and her siblings followed their mother to her huge three-foot-high storehouses of cones. Her excitement and her chittering conveyed to her youngsters the importance of storing food.

At the end of July the chickaree left home. She scurried down the mountain running along the limbs of one forest tree to the next.

Occasionally she scurried over the ground. Ravens chased her, hawks pursued her, and other chickarees screamed at her when she crossed their property. Finally she arrived on this small patch of land on the shores of the Bitterroot River. She climbed the big hemlock. No red squirrels chased or screamed at her. She had found a home. It was a good home, rich with cone-bearing trees: Douglas firs, hemlocks, lodgepole pines, and a white spruce.

Immediately, she built herself hideouts. They were nests of sticks and leaves in which to hide when the pine martens, her deadly enemies, were hunting her. She ate flower and grass seeds, cones, berries, mushrooms, insects, and sometimes bird eggs. She laid out highways through the trees, and she chittered and screeched constantly. When she had built safe places to hide, she started her storehouse.

When the spruce cones were large and

green and the lodgepole pine cones were ripe, she was a busy chickaree. She ran to every part of her property, including the highest tree-tops and the forest floor. She sat on stumps peeling cones and eating the seeds. The left-overs she put in her storehouse. She worked all day long and even in the moonlight when the owls were hunting.

She cut and dropped green cones to the ground, then put them in the water so they would not dry out and shed their seeds. Mushrooms and toadstools she laid in the sun to dry. She buried berries in pine needles to preserve them, and all the while she chit-tered and clucked.

While she worked, she scolded the jays, the pack rats, the mice, the woodpeckers, and the nuthatches—all the creatures that came to steal from her storehouse.

And she screeched most ferociously at the marten who included her property in his own home range of seven square miles. He did not want her food; he wanted her.

In November her cousin moved into the half acre right next to hers, and she devoted much of her time to scolding him. His land was not as rich as hers, and he would sneak over their border and steal from her storehouse. Some foods she buried in the ground to protect them from this marauder.

When the cold winds howled and the leaves blew off the willows and cottonwoods along the river, the chickaree built herself a winter nest in the dense foliage at the top of a Douglas fir. She made it both windproof and rainproof with leaves, pine needles, moss, and dry twigs. Cleverly designed, it was about twenty inches wide and several feet deep. The room inside was lined with insulating rootlets and soft plant fibers. During December and January, when the snow locked up the valley of the Bitterroot, she spent much of her time sleeping in her cozy winter home—unless a trespasser came on her land—and then she was awake and chittering. Toward the end of February she stopped screaming and took a mate.

When the white starflowers opened and the fragrant balsamroot flowered in the first week in April, she left her winter home and her mate and moved into the black-backed woodpecker's abandoned home in a big Douglas fir tree. She lined the cavity with fibers and soft needles. Then, as the early birds arrived from South America and the fish snapped miller moths off the surface of the river, she gave birth.

Unlike the chickaree, some property owners shared. Across the river in the grass on the sagebrush flats, the sage grouse held community land. It was a stage used by all the members of their group. On it the males danced, displaying to the females their gorgeous feathers and the wondrous yellow air sacs on their necks.

On the day the chickaree babies were born, a male grouse ran across the dance floor as fast as he could go. His spiked tail was spread over his back. He dragged his wings to show off the beautiful white feathers on his rump. He lifted his neck feathers and the bright-yellow comb over his eyes. He was magnificent. Another male ran out to meet him. They vibrated their tails and drummed their quills like castanets. They closed their eyes and danced in a trance. Eventually the first male peeked at his rival, saw he still had his eyes closed, and sneaked away. The second male opened his eyes, saw he was foolishly alone and also ran. All this day and the next and the next for weeks, pairs of male grouse would meet on the community stage. The females would seem not to be watching the show-offs, but they would be. Later, nests in the grasses with eight to twelve grouse eggs would attest to their interest.

The chickaree did not hear the sage grouse drum that morning. She was licking her babies to stimulate their hearts and lungs. When they were dry and breathing softly, she rested her head in her doorway and peered down at the river shore. The yellow holly grapes that grew close to the ground bloomed in the sunshine, and the golden flowers of the glacier lilies nodded in the wind. Their appearance meant the eggs of the bald eagles were about to hatch, and that the bighorn sheep were lambing.

The chickaree watched everything on the riverbank, for she was curious as well as noisy. She saw the magpie pick up a stick and show it to his mate, and she saw the mate lift her feathers in approval. Next, the magpie carried it to a cottonwood and put it in a tree crotch. It was the first of many sticks that would make up their nest.

While they worked, the chickaree dropped off to sleep, curled around her babies.

"Tshee, tsheee, tshee!" She awoke in surprise. A tree swallow hovered at her door. Just back from the coast of the Gulf of Mexico, the bird was peeking into every hole in the forest to see if it would make a suitable nest.

"TCHER-r-r-r," the chickaree screamed. The hole was definitely occupied. The swallow flew off.

A rustle sounded in the dry fir needles on the ground, and the chickaree looked down. Chewing at a biscuitroot plant was a field mouse. The chickaree ignored it, but the pine marten did not. He ran down from a tree, caught it, and ate it.

As the chickaree babies grew, the mother spent more time away from them. One morning she was stuffing seeds in her cheeks when she heard the *"killie killie"* of the kestrel, the smallest North American falcon. Only a week before, this colorful bird had returned from his wintering grounds in the south.

At first he had sat quietly on a tree stump, flying out to catch insects, then returning to look over his old home. In a few days he, too, felt the moon of April and began defending his property against neighboring kestrels. His nest would not be ready for another two weeks; his young would not hatch until June.

Farther up the riverbank, the red-tailed hawk warmed her eggs. Every three hours the female stood up on her stick nest and carefully turned them with her beak to keep the embryos from sticking to the shells. Then she sat down and relaxed into the broody silence of incubation, not hearing, not even seeing the lovely snowdrops and blue-eyed Marys bobbing all across the meadow before her.

The night that the full moon of April rose over the valley of the Bitterroot River, the mother chickaree squirmed and tossed. Her babies had grown so big, they were crowding her out of the hollow. She gave up and went to sleep in a crotch of the tree.

At dawn the babies awoke to hear their mother screaming at a coyote, then at her cousin, then at the magpie. Another April morning had begun. The mother nursed her youngsters and ran down the tree.

She did not stop until she reached the spruce cones she had stored in the water last fall. Pulling one out, she carried it to a stump and peeled the sheaths off the seeds and ate them. She ran up the hemlock where she had hidden dried huckleberries and hastily ate some of them. Then she checked her big storehouse, screamed to tell her cousin to stay away, and dashed off to eat buds in the cottonwood where the magpies had built their nest. The magpies dived and raged at her, for red squirrels are not above eating birds' eggs. She ducked their blows, then ran down the tree and into her forest.

Her day was just beginning. She scurried up

a lodgepole pine and looked in a hole where she had stored edible fungi. It was occupied by a black-backed woodpecker, who instantly flew at her. Jumping to a twig, she trapezed to a limb and crawled under a piece of hanging bark. Safe, she watched the woodpecker fly by.

The moon of the property owners' shenanigans kept the mother chickaree busy. One day she took her favorite highway through the trees to see if her cousin was at her stream. Suddenly, the trail ended in empty space. An aspen tree was missing. It had been cut down during the night by the beaver who slept in his lodge in the middle of his pond. The tree was now his property, not hers. When his mate, who was curled over their four newborn kits, had eaten her fill of the aspen bark, he would carry the tree to the dam and use it to raise the water level.

Finding no cousin, she circled the property. As she approached her storehouse, she heard chewing sounds. Someone was robbing her! She dashed to the top of her food pile.

"*TCHERR-r-r-r-rrrrrrrrrrrrrrrrrrrr*," she screeched. A pack rat had a cone in her mouth. Hearing the angry chickaree, she ran ten yards to her own castle. Still carrying the cone, the rat slipped into a huge pile of sticks and grass and dropped her booty beside her most cherished possessions——a bottle top, a fish hook, and one shiny dime she had found by the river.

The pack rat cuddled around her fifteen-day-old young and went to sleep, her nose touching the cone that was now her property.

The chickaree was still scolding. When she became quiet, a thieving chickadee took a seed from her storehouse. Several young mice stuck their heads out of the tunnels they had made in it. Mice in a storehouse are a disaster. They would eat everything. She was torn. It was time to feed her babies, but she must save her property.

In frustration, she scolded for seven long minutes, then stopped. The forest was quiet, the mice nowhere to be seen. Wearily she climbed up her tree toward her family. She had hardly gone halfway when she saw the magpie fly to her toadstool supply.

"*TCHERRRRR*." The chickaree was about to chase the bird when she heard her babies cry. The sound pulled her up the tree as if she were on a string. The moon of property owners' rights was also the moon of nurturing. She flicked her fuzzy tail and slipped into the hollow.

No sooner were her babies fed and cleaned than she was off again to check on her property. She must defend it. The lives of her offspring depended on it.

The magpie was now in the water, bathing at the edge of the river. He was nervously watching the sky. Suddenly he cried his alarm note and flew into the cottonwood.

The chickaree had learned that the birds, with their keen eyesight, saw enemies long before she did. She ran into a nearby hideout. A golden eagle came into view, his wings motionless as he rode the air current above the river. Here was a real enemy.

"*RRRRRRR!*" she warned. Every bird stopped what he was doing and sat perfectly still. Eagles see movement. Birds somehow know that if they do not move, eagles and other predators will not see them.

"*TCHERRrrrrrrrrrrrrrrrrrr!*" The chickaree awoke the pine marten, who was sleeping at the top of a spruce tree.

The large slender marten, whose beautiful fur is known as sable, moved with sensuous grace. Chickarees were one of his favorite foods. He looked for the screamer, could not find her, and came down the tree like flowing water. He was met by another marten, who was passing through. The two males did not fight, for martens share their property with their own kind. The males have several mates, who raise the young by themselves in hollow logs and under fallen trees.

The woodpecker, who was drilling into a dead pine, saw the martens. *"Yk,"* he warned, and circled to the other side of the trunk so they could not see him. The chickaree heard this alarm and stayed where she was. The strange marten went up the mountain and the other ran to the marsh where the moose was browsing.

A hooded merganser saw the marten and swam into the grass, his black-and-white head now looking like sunshine and shadow. The marten did not see the bird.

The tree swallows saw the hunter and spread out over the river calling, *"CHI-veet,"* their alarm note.

Finding nothing to eat in the marsh, the marten circled back into the forest and climbed to a tree limb, still looking for the chickaree.

Gathering his short, powerful legs under him, he leaped twenty feet to the limb of another tree. It was the chickaree's nursery tree. He climbed to the top and hid in its dense needles to wait for her.

The chickaree did not leave her hideout until she heard a pine siskin, a song sparrow, and finally a lazuli bunting sing. The caroling of the birds meant that there was no enemy to be seen. She ran out into the sunlight and back to her babies so swiftly that the dozing marten caught only a fleeting glimpse of her tail as she disappeared in her hole.

Safe, she listened to the male songbirds mark their property lines with songs. Birds tell other males of their kind not to trespass by singing. Melodies are their swords.

Along the river a western tanager had a problem. He had returned from the south to find a strange male on his last summer's property. This was not tolerable, because when his mate returned in a few days, she would take the male who owned the property as her partner, not him.

To prevent this, the tanager flew to a bush and faced his opponent. He lifted his feathers to make himself twice as big as he was. This frightened the rival, but he did not fly away. The tanager vibrated his wings. Finally he thrust out his beak, a sight as terrifying to a bird as that of someone pointing a gun toward a person.

The rival could bear it no longer. He gave up and flew down the river to find a piece of unoccupied land.

When he departed, the tanager threw back his head and warbled his property song over and over again.

The chickaree put her head out her doorway. She was ready to start off again. The marten tensed his muscles to spring. At that moment a baby fussed and the mother dropped out of sight to console it.

"*TCHEEEEr,*" her cousin yelled. With that she dashed from her hollow and ran down the tree so fast, the marten did not have time to leap. However, he followed her to her storehouse.

In a rock crevice about two feet from the storehouse a rattlesnake was coiled. His heart-shaped head swung slowly on his arched neck. The snake had just come out of his hibernation and was warming himself in the sunlight. He was still cold. He moved slowly, and the chickaree saw him.

"*TCHERRRRRRRRRR,*" she screamed. She jumped onto a low tree limb and rode with it down, then up, leaped to a higher limb and got away. The cousin saw the snake and froze in fright. The marten pounced on him.

That evening the chickaree did not hear her cousin. His poor property had forced him to trespass once too often.

Toward the end of April, the gray jay came

The salamander comes to the edge
of the woodland pond.

The salamander swims
beneath a gathering of fairy shrimp.

Marlene Hill Werner

To reach the underside of a rock,
the salamander follows a secret trail.

After several days,
young chickarees can jump from limb to limb.

A pack rat hides his most prized possessions
under a huge pile of sticks.

Kam Mak

The trees become spectacles of beauty
as butterflies alight.

Kam Mak

Eating constantly,
the caterpillar grows rapidly, then creates a chrysalis,
where miraculous changes take place.

A milkweed plant attracts the monarch butterfly.

to the river for a treat. Thousands of caterpillars were abroad. They rippled and humped as they climbed twigs and plants. The jay stabbed at one. The caterpillar reared its head and tail and curled into a circle. It looked so much like a bud that the bird did not recognize it as food. He hopped toward another caterpillar.

In the last days of April, the swallows were treated to a feast. The black flies hatched and flew over the river in dark clouds. All winter these insects had clung to submerged rocks in their larval stage. They looked like little palm trees, the "leaves" of which paddled food into their mouths. When the "palm trees" split open, the adults emerged inside bubbles of air. In these they floated to the surface, opened their new wings, and flew. Then the tree swallows feasted.

On the last day of the April moon, the jay called his mate to join him at the storehouse.

The chickaree came on the run and found them eating her seeds.

This was too much to bear!

She climbed to her winter home, which was right above the storehouse, tidied it up, and rushed back to her hollow. Picking up a furry baby in her teeth, she carried it down the trunk, over the ground, and up to the winter nest. She laid it carefully inside, then went back for another and another.

When all four were gathered in the home above the storehouse, the mother chickaree looked down contentedly. At last she could fulfill all the rites of the April moon with one scolding.

A good loud *TCHERRRRRRRRRRR-r-r-r-r-r-r* from the top of the tree would protect both her young and her property. No one embodied the spirit of the April moon like the chickaree.

THE MOON OF THE
MONARCH BUTTERFLIES

The moon of May slipped below the curve of the earth a few minutes before dawn. Darkness engulfed the long, wide Mississippi River Valley.

In a damp field in Arkansas, in the brief blackness before daybreak, a dewy breeze arose. Scented with wet loam, sassafras leaves, and sweet-scented shrub, it blew through the woods and over a rice field, and faded in the river thickets. Then the sun came up.

Where the breeze had traveled, swatches of wildflowers were blooming. Violets, May apples, and columbine bounced on cool green stems; dogbanes, wild geraniums, irises, and buttercups sprang toward the sun. Apple flowers blossomed. Their petals fell like paper snowstorms. Pine and pecan blooms released their pollen, and the winged seeds on the maples spun as they ripened. The warm moist earth of May and the lengthening hours of light were renewing life all across North America.

The longer days triggered the birds to migrate. As far up the Mississippi River as Iowa, a sky tide of wings rolled northward night and day. They were the migrants that arrive on their nesting grounds in May—the bluebirds, warblers, thrushes, flycatchers, wrens, and orioles. A few days behind them came the indigo buntings and cuckoos, meadowlarks and spotted sandpipers. All the birds were flying in uncountable billions toward trees, grasslands, seashores, or little wooden boxes on poles—their summer nesting places. This migration that had begun slowly in January and February was now at its height. Ribbons of wings streamed over the Mississippi River Valley and the Atlantic and Pacific coastlines, which are the sky roads, called flyways, of the birds.

Beneath the birds, flying strong on paper-thin wings, went another migrant—a monarch butterfly. She had left her winter home in Mexico, flown across Texas, and was now traveling northeast on a straight line through Arkansas. She flew across open fields, over blooming peach trees and greening vineyards. She was on her way home to the faraway place in which she had been born—a meadowland near Toronto in Ontario, Canada.

The monarch had been flying for many days. This morning she had soared and flapped forty miles, crossing into Missouri at noon. She winged on, passing the smokestacks of Poplar Bluff, its shopping centers, churches, and railroad station. Before sundown she came to rest on a wisteria vine that entwined the porch of a small white house in the country. Clinging to a lavender flower, she closed her wings above her back, as butterflies do. Her wing tops were burnt orange, their undersides yellow. Black veins spread through them like lead in a stained-glass window. Their edges seemed as if the night and day had been knitted into them; they sparkled white and black. Her antennae were club-tipped wands that could smell flowers, feel obstacles, and help to orient her in flight.

The monarch was not as brilliant as she had been in September, when she had changed from her pupal stage into a butterfly. She had then set out on her long migration south, from Canada to the Lava Mountains of Mexico. There in a warm, moist forest she had overwintered with millions of other monarch butterflies, then started home to Canada.

The long flight had taken its toll on her. One wing was slightly torn, and many of the scales that colored her body and wings had fallen away. Although she looked more fragile than when she had started, her pale wings and body were still incredibly strong and could easily carry her home.

Just before evening the butterfly sipped nectar from the wisteria flowers on the porch, uncurling her proboscis as she reached deep into their sweet pots. Then she rested. She was alone, for the spring migration of monarch butterflies is not as social as their autumnal flight, when thousands fly by day and gather together at night.

This journey begins when the coolness nips the land. Those butterflies that emerge before the killing frost of autumn take wing and hurry like leaves before the wind. Down the east and west coasts they fly by the millions along the ancient, invisible sky trails of the monarchs. Many go eighty miles before floating down to a tree to rest away the night with others of their species. The trees they choose are usually pines, maples, or willows— trees where their tiny feet can cling to the slender needles or the small notches in the leaves. As the butterflies gather, the trees become spectacles of beauty. Firelike wings seem to set them aflame. They flicker yellow and orange. Once a tree is visited by monarchs, it becomes a butterfly tree and they may visit it every year—nobody knows how this knowledge is passed on.

At dawn the wisteria vine where the butterfly rested became a noisy place. Several dozen house sparrows chirped and fluttered their wings as they awoke. Their untidy nests, crammed into the dense vines, were filled with cheeping babies whose feathers were just breaking out of their stubby sheaths. The butterfly could not see the birds, for the sun was not bright enough to bring vision to her eyes. Each of her eyes is really thousands of eyes that make up one compound eye.

When at last she could see the flowers and sky, she opened her wings and flew. Soaring over a tall magnolia tree, she looked down on fading pink blossoms that once stood like china cups on short stems. Now the petals were falling to earth.

She did not stop to drink magnolia nectar, but she did sense it on the air with her proboscis, antennae, and feet, for these parts of the butterfly are its taste buds.

Still flying northeast, she came to Cape Girardeau in Missouri.

Below her in the marshy edges of the big Mississippi River, the eggs of spring peepers were hatching: Tiny polliwogs twisted and flipped as they broke through their egg cases and the walls of gelatin that had protected them while they developed. Free but tired, they sank to the food-filled bottom of the shallows.

In deeper water a male sunfish was just beginning to form his nest. He was sweeping the silt from a sandy bar, using his tail and fins as a broom. The butterfly did not see him or the ripple on the water made by his female as she circled down to examine his glittering saucer-shaped nest. In a few days she would lay her eggs there, then swim away, leaving her mate to guard them from enemies and keep them clean of silt until they hatched. The fine sediment can smother and kill fish eggs.

Flying hard now, staying about twenty feet above the ground, the butterfly flew around factories and granaries, glided over houses and puddled country roads. She glanced down at the designs in the fields, looking for a very special shape and color—a milkweed plant. She came lower, feeling the pressure of an egg within her, an egg that must be laid on a milk-weed and no other plant. The caterpillar that would hatch from it could eat no other food.

A male awaited her in a milkweed patch. She mated with him and flew deep into the patch. A tiny yolk within her was now covered with a strong shell in which there was a minus-cule hole.

The butterfly alighted on the oval leaf of a young milkweed growing beside a country road. She folded her wings above her back. As an egg left her body, it passed her sperm receptacle and was fertilized by way of the hole in the egg's shell. About as big as half a pinhead, the egg adhered to the leaf's under-surface. It glittered, for it was multifaceted, like a diamond. The butterfly left it on the leaf and flew on.

In a few days the egg on the milkweed would hatch. A tiny caterpillar, lavishly banded with white and greenish yellow, would open its jaws, feed on the eggshell, and bite into the tender leaf.

Eating almost constantly, the caterpillar would grow rapidly. In a few days its coat would split down its back and the caterpillar would step out of it a little larger and a little brighter in color. Now it would have black bands as well as the white and yellow ones. This molt would happen four times. At the last molt, usually after fourteen days, the caterpillar would be approximately two inches long.

This larger and more colorful caterpillar would walk under a leaf on which it had been feeding. There it would spin and attach a silken pad to the leaf stem and grasp it with its two false rear legs that exist only in the caterpillar stage to hold up its long body. Letting go with its true front legs, it would hang downward in a J shape. Violently twisting, the caterpillar would shed its fifth coat, and there would be no more caterpillar.

In its place would be a green-gold case, studded with golden jewellike spots. In this—the chrysalis—the monarch butterfly would begin a miraculous change. Legs, head, and body would be reorganized.

After two weeks, the insect inside the case would turn dark red and the chrysalis coat would split. A delicate black leg would reach out. A pert head with big eyes and a coiled proboscis would emerge. Finally, the graceful insect, now splashed with black and white, would crawl out on the chrysalis and lift wing buds that look much like the buds of flowers. The monarch would pump fluid into the buds, and they would unfold into four beautiful wings. When they dried, the monarch would fly, drink nectar, mate, and, if it was a female, bejewel the milkweed plants with the summer eggs of the species. Unlike her migrating mother, she would live only a few months.

It is the butterflies of August and September

that live long lives—up to six months. They are the migrants. They must live through the winter in a moist warm climate in order to perpetuate their species. When they start off for their southern homes, they are not sexually developed; nevertheless, the sex of each migrant can be distinguished. The males have one black spot on each of their hind wings.

The migrants take a bearing on the sun to find their way. They look at the angle of light, turn, and lift their antenna. Then they take off on a beam that leads to their winter homes. In the west they fly from Canada down the coastal mountains to Palm Grove, California. In the east they travel from Canada and the eastern United States on a perfectly straight line to the Lava Mountains near Mexico City. Practically no monarchs live on the dry plains and midlands of the United States and Canada.

Having deposited her egg, the monarch took off to the northeast. She darted through a park near the outskirts of Evansville, Indiana, on the Ohio River. A boy jumped to catch her. She climbed away from him and skimmed the treetops. A wind blew her to the docks where people worked and back out over the water where barges and fishing boats moved.

Before dusk the butterfly saw the white line of a ship's railing below her. She dropped down to rest, not knowing she was hitching a ride up the Ohio River.

She closed her wings over her back. Along the quiet edges of the river where the water was shallow and moved slowly, bullhead catfish had gathered in couples to spawn and renew life. Some were making nests in the bank, digging with their mouths. They were picking up silt and spewing it into the current to be carried away. Other catfish couples had already laid eggs. Some nests were beside old logs, others in the round caves of sunken automobile tires.

One pair of parents was guarding a cluster of little black hatchlings inside a tire. As tiny as they were—about the size of a fly's leg—they looked like miniatures of their parents. Their faces were adorned with whiskers. Their back fins were oval, their skin slippery and seemingly scaleless. The tiny fish had lines down their bodies. These were their balancing organs and ears. Called lateral lines, they told the fish whether they were right side up or not. The lines also picked up distant sounds—a crayfish moving stones, an eel swishing down to eat them.

An hour later, when twilight darkened the water, the father catfish nosed his children out of the tire. He followed the wheeling cluster as they went out into the weeds to feed. A hungry bass came toward them. The catfish father opened his jaws and sucked his fry into his mouth. He held them there until the bass swam on by. He would tend them in this manner until they were almost a half inch long; then he would swim away and leave them to fend for themselves. Even he would not recognize his offspring after they were independent. If they passed too closely, he would swallow them.

The monarch rode on up the Ohio River. Overhead hot and cold air collided, clouds formed, and rain splattered on the river and the valley. The butterfly crept under the boat railing and spent the rainy night clinging to a splinter by the hooks on the tips of her feet.

At dawn the boat pulled into the dock at New Albany, Indiana. The storm was over. The hills were wet with rain shine. Bright azaleas, which had already bloomed and faded in Arkansas, were still flowering in cooler Indiana. Tree leaves were smaller here, for the warmth moved slowly up the continent.

The butterfly crawled up on the railing and found her position had changed in the night. She took another reading on the sun and flew toward the awakening town. She was back on course. She fluttered around the downtown buildings, flew on to the outlying railroad yards, and kept going. When she saw green patches of farmland below her, she came earthward.

A bluebird flew toward her. She was hunting insects for her young, but when she saw the black and orange colors, the bird darted away. The monarch butterfly is poisonous to birds, and they have learned to avoid it. The bluebird swerved and caught a crane fly. Alighting on a fence post, she slipped into a hole. A lusty chattering and chirping greeted the parent. Red mouths opened, and the bluebird fed one lively nestling. The babies almost filled the hollow in the post, for they were fully feathered and ready to fly. Bluebirds nest early. Their babies would be taking short flights when the wood thrushes and orioles were still building their nests in mid-May.

Near a red barn a vegetable garden was striped with the green sprouts of cucumbers and squashes. The first thick leaves of the melon plants stood boldy in the sun. Hard green strawberries gleamed among fringed leaves. Beyond the garden the rye was beginning to flower. The corn had just been planted.

The butterfly again flew down to lay another egg. Dropping among the blades of the foxtail grass, she found a young milkweed plant, laid an egg, and flew off into the wind. She passed a woods where a loose cluster of paper wasps was hovering around an elm limb. A small cluster of egg cells marked the beginning of their home. A few of the wasps had gathered the fibers of plants and were chewing them into a tough material for more egg cells. Others were converting wood fiber into the gray paper that would encircle the wasp eggs like a castle wall.

Deeper in the woods the flowers of the tulip trees were sitting on short stems like orange-green fruit cups. The walnut and butternut trees were fragrant with spicy yellow-green flowers, and the feathery blossoms of the willows were drifting on the wind like a cloud of goose down.

A southwesterly breeze carried the butterfly on to the northeast. She soared over wild cherry trees where robins and blue jays were harvesting the first of the ripening fruit. She flew over roads that were bordered with blue wild phlox.

The next day she was southwest of Dayton, Ohio, and still flying northeast. A small milkweed plant attracted her, and she fluttered down upon it to lay another egg. The morning was warm, almost eighty degrees, and she was thirsty. She flitted to a flower and drank its nectar. Refreshed, she sailed above a dirt road that led through a hardwood forest of hickories, oaks, maples, and ashes.

A long-tailed weasel darted among the trees looking from right to left with quick flashes of her golden head. She had a long graceful neck and bright black eyes. Her belly was white, the tip of her tail black. In her mouth hung a baby, curled like a bud, its head tucked into its feet. Its eyes had opened only that day. Although it had been born in early April, it was not until this thirty-seventh day of its life that it could see. By the end of the May moon it would be weaned and, in a few more weeks, hunting mice and frogs on its own.

The mother weasel saw no dangers and carried her little one under the ferns and trillium leaves without stirring them. She emerged on the stream bank. Flowing over the stones, she disappeared into a den she had fashioned only last night. Early that evening she had felt a need to move her family and had made this den by the stream. The food was more plentiful by the waterway. She put the baby in a leaf-lined nest deep in the embankment and went back for the others. When all were moved, she slept beside them, waiting until darkness to hunt food. She would move them again and again before they were independent.

As the butterfly flew along the road, a baby cottontail, no bigger than a human fist, came bounding out from under a bush. The cottontail hopped to the woodland meadow to nibble a flowering chickweed. As she munched, three bright faces watched. The red fox's pups, still fuzzy with baby fur, still wobbly and awkward, studied the little cottontail. From the safe darkness of their den at the edge of the woods, they watched everything that moved—bees, birds, wind-blown flowers—and the cottontail. Presently they crawled back into their earthen den, for they were still too young to venture into the woods.

The woodland also hid skunk babies. One family was curled in the hollow of a fallen tree. Only three days old, the babies were covered with black fuzz. On their backs could clearly be seen the white stripe of the skunk.

In the chamber of another woodland den, four baby chipmunks sat on their haunches near their mother. She gave them a signal, and with a bound, they ran up the long tunnel that led from their bedroom to the sunlight at the surface. They climbed onto a log, tails up like flagpoles, and boxed each other with their front paws. Then they rushed into the woods to stuff fallen maple seeds into their cheeks. Born in March, they were now six weeks old and being weaned. Their mother was nursing them less and less, so they went farther and farther from home to investigate the woods and hunt for seeds and berries. This morning one stayed away until noon, then ran home with a cheekful of cherry seeds.

The butterfly flew on. She climbed above the forest and flew northeast until late afternoon. When the light grew too dim for her to see, she came to rest in a pine tree near a blue-fruited dogwood blooming in an abandoned field. The needles rustled, and a catbird landed on a limb below her. He jumped to another branch, then straightened his feathers and wiped his bill on a twig. He, too, had been traveling all day. In a last dash to get home to his abandoned field, he had flown two hundred miles. He was not out of breath, nor did his heart pound from the exertion of his long trip. His body, like the bodies of all birds, made adjustments to the demands of migration. He was feeling fine. He flitted into the center of the pine and listened to his woodland neighbors.

The green frogs were piping their evening song, and the wood thrush, which had arrived only a few days before, called out his first song of the season. Like the spilling of water, the clear notes of this beautiful bird poured forth. Then, at sundown, the wood thrush stopped singing. From a tall tree a phoebe called in the dusk. Presently, he too was quiet. The robins chirped on, then suddenly stopped. Each kind of bird has a curfew of light that silences it for the night. First the wood thrush is quiet, then the phoebe and robin. Finally, when these are silent, the pensive sweet carol of the wood pewee begins in the afterglow. When the song is done, it is night.

Darkness had come many hours ago for the butterfly, and she could not see the glow of the firefly in the grass blades below her. A female had turned on the light in the last four segments of her abdomen. Nearby, a male walked across a leaf. He did not glow, for he had just emerged from his pupal stage. His wings were small, his body fragile. He was not mature enough to shine. It would be late June before he would sparkle two consecutive flashes, the mating call of his species. He walked to the end of the leaf and rested.

The night passed quietly for the butterfly. When the May moon was setting and the sun coming over the edge of the world, the wood pewee began his song of the predawn. Next came the voices of the robin, the cardinal, the phoebe, and the wood thrush as, one by one, the birds awoke to their morning light alarm. The catbird listened and joyfully imitated them all.

A song sparrow saluted the morning with a soft song. In a nest in a bush his mate was brooding five downy babies no bigger than peanuts. He kept his song low so as not to attract predators to them.

For sixteen days the male had guarded the nest while the female sat on their eggs and warmed them. She departed only to eat.

There were many other birds with babies

in the woods and fields. The young mourning doves were almost as large as their parents, and under the bridge the phoebe babies were looking over the edge of their nest.

Out in the field young killdeer were flying with their parents. They had taken to their wings a few hours after hatching, for killdeer are precocious at birth. On the limb of a pine by a bridge sat four young screech owls. Their heads were still wispy with puffs of down, and their breasts were streaked with the gray of owl childhood, but they were very much on their own. At night they hunted the young mice and fat June beetles; by day, when not sleeping, they watched the fledglings of the prairie horned larks take long gliding trips over the grass tops. Hatched in late March, the little larks were flying while their parents made a nest in the alfalfa field for another brood.

As the daytime animals awoke and became

busy, the butterfly crawled into the sunlight. When she could see the meadow and trees, she opened her wings and flew on.

She passed over ponds in Ohio where the young salamanders were breaking out of their egg cases and swimming among the plant stems. Gills, like ruffs, stood out from their necks, distinguishing them from frog tadpoles.

All that afternoon the monarch flew over Lake Erie and finally arrived in Canada. She came to a railroad bed where the milkweed was abundant, and here in the land where monarchs abound, she laid the last of her eggs. Toward dusk she fluttered to a pine tree by a freshwater marsh and rested.

May was not far along here. The yellow cowslips were just blooming. The arrowhead leaves were still uncurling their points to the sun, and only a few leaves of the yellow pond lilies had grown to the surface, where they would flatten on the water like paper plates. The azaleas were in bud, and the apple trees had yet to blossom.

At dusk a cheerful May chorus filled the air. Male American hop toads were singing. Their voices were tremulous and sweet as they blew their throats into tan balloons bigger than their heads. They sang for several seconds, then stopped abruptly in the manner of hop toads. The female toads listened as they sat quietly under ferns and among the new leaves of the wintergreen. Female toads do not sing; however, inspired by the chorus, one female jumped into the water. A male clasped her with his front feet, and together they drifted among the sunken sticks and leaves. The female laid a ribbon of thousands of eggs while the sperm from the male flowed over and fertilized them.

Frogs were calling, too. The tree frogs trilled, and once a bullfrog croaked. He rumbled like thunder but then stopped, for it was too early for his June courtship song.

The next day the butterfly flew on. Her wings were now small and dry. As fluids had flowed from her body into her eggs, she had shriveled. She flew slowly as she traveled beneath the tide of warblers and thrushes returning to Canada.

A wind blew her to the shores of Lake Ontario. The tatter in her wing tore deeper. Sea gulls, incubating eggs in vast colonies on the sand dunes, tilted their heads and looked up at her. Terns and sandpipers paid her no heed as they ran in and out of the lapping water hunting small sand crabs.

The butterfly was nearly home. She had almost reached the meadow where she had been born, when suddenly a gust of wind carried her out over Lake Ontario. Her life done, she folded her wings and floated like a flower petal onto the waves.

Night came. The May moon climbed the sky. From Missouri to Canada the heirs and heiresses of the butterfly's beautiful life were beginning her story again under the moon of renewal.

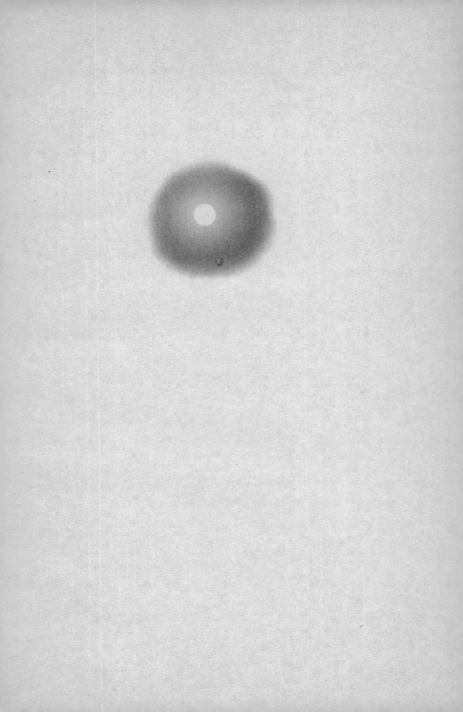

BIBLIOGRAPHY

Billings, Charlene W. *Salamanders*. New York: Dodd, Mead, 1981.

————. *Salamanders as Pets*. New York: Dodd, Mead, 1981.

Bishop, Sherman C. *Handbook of Salamanders*. New York: Hafner Publishing Company, 1962.

Brennan, Gale. *Earl, the Squirrel*. Chicago: Children's Press, 1980.

Carter, Anne. *Scurry's Treasure*. New York: Crown Publishers, 1987.

Cochran, Doris M. *Living Amphibians of the World*. Garden City, N.Y.: Doubleday & Company, 1961.

Coldrey, Jennifer. *The World of Squirrels*. Milwaukee, Wis.: Gareth Stevens, Inc., 1986.

Compton's Encyclopedia. Vol. 22, p. 25. Chicago: Encyclopedia Britannica Inc., 1980.

Conant, Roger. *A Field Guide to Reptiles and Amphibians of Eastern and Central North America.* Boston: Houghton Miflin Company, 1975.

Davis, Adrian. *Discovering Squirrels.* Mankato, Minn.: Crestwood House, 1983.

Gibbons, Gail. *Monarch Butterfly.* New York: Holiday House, 1989.

Heberman, Ethan. *The Great Butterfly Hunt.* New York: Simon & Schuster, 1990.

Lepthien, Emilie U. *Monarch Butterflies.* Chicago: Children's Press, 1989.

Martin, Alexander C., Herbert Zim, and Arnold L. Nelson. *American Wildlife and Plants: A Guide to Wildlife Food Habits.* New York: Dover Publications, Inc., 1951.

McConoughey, Jana. *The Squirrels.* Mankato, Minn.: Crestwood House, 1983.

Morgan, Ann Haven. *Field Book of Ponds and Streams.* New York: G. P. Putnam's Sons, 1930.

Norsgaard, Jaediker E. *How to Raise Butterflies.* New York: Putnam Press, 1988.

Palmer, Ralph S. *The Mammal Guide.* Garden City, N.Y.: Doubleday & Company, 1954.

Patent, Dorothy Winshaw. *Butterflies and Moths: How They Function.* New York: Holiday House, 1979.

St. Tamara. *Chickaree: A Red Squirrel.* Orlando, Fla.: Harcourt Brace Jovanovich, 1980.

Stanley, Colleen. *Tree Squirrels.* New York: Dodd, Mead, 1983.

Terry, Trevor. *The Life Cycle of a Butterfly.* New York: Bookwright Press, 1988.

Thompson, Susan L. *Diary of a Monarch Butterfly.* New York: Magic Circle Press, 1976.

Urquhart, Frederick A. *The Monarch Butterfly: International Traveler.* Chicago: Nelson-Hall, 1987.

Van Wormer, Joe. *Squirrels.* New York: E. P. Dutton, 1978.

Watts, Barrie. *Butterfly and Caterpillar*. Morristown, N.J.: Silver Burdett, 1986.

The World Book Encyclopedia. Vol. 17, p. 53. Chicago: World Book Inc., 1983.

INDEX

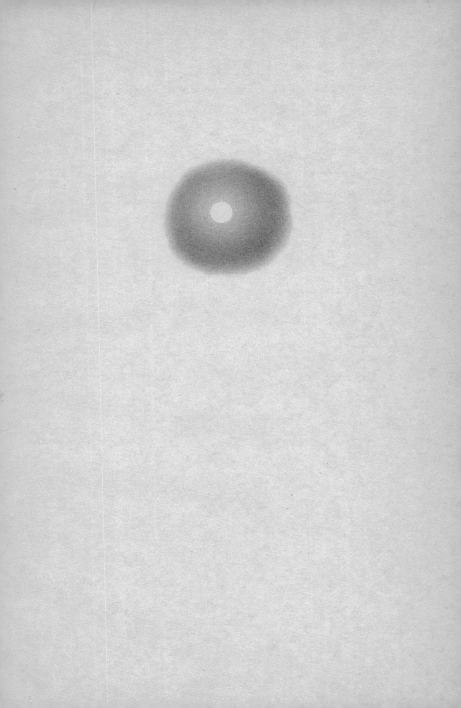